To Dan! HAPPY BIRTHDAY
I know your a Russian Spy!
love you always, Mary :)

1997

Russia
—and Beyond

Photography by Nick Gheissari

Text by Patricia Raine

A colorfully faceted dome atop the Church of the Resurrection of Christ overlooks the spectacular city of St. Petersburg. Built on the very spot where Tsar Alexander II was assassinated in 1881, the site is also known, memorially, as the Church of the Saviour on the Spilled Blood.

Preface

ON DECEMBER 25, 1991, THE POWERFUL AND ENIGMATIC Union of Soviet Socialist Republics finally and irrevocably split apart. In the turbulent years since that dissolution, the rest of the world has witnessed the stunning metamorphosis of Russia and its former satellites.

Today, the autonomous countries of Russia, Ukraine, Belarus, and those of the Baltics, the Caucasus, and Central Asia cautiously co-exist—determined to accommodate this very public re-invention while retaining their greater heritage and particular cultures.

Herein lies a portrait of that ongoing transformation towards independence by photographer Nick Gheissari. His celebratory vision, five years in the making, reveals an old land entering a new era and portrays a vivid, resilient people standing in the light of this great change—newly emerged from the shadow of the Iron Curtain.

ACKNOWLEDGMENTS

This book came to be through the talents and encouragement of several special people.

First, my grateful thanks to the graphic design team of Bono Mitchell and Tom Specht for their enduring patience and beautifully conceived page layouts—the perfect context for these photographs. My gratitude also to writer Patricia Raine for transforming my effusive narratives into paragraphs of substance and grace.

I want to extend a very special thank-you to His Excellency Yuli Vorontsov, the Russian Ambassador to the United States, for graciously hosting the first exhibition of the photographs in December of 1994, at the Russian Embassy in Washington, D.C.

In addition, my acknowledgments go to Dena Glading for her selfless love and support, to Matthew Fletcher and Sherry Bahktiar for lending their minds and energies to this project, and to all of my friends for their support of my vision as a photographer.

In Moscow, my friends George Skryabin, Anna Kozlovsky, and Lena Nikoleava bolstered my efforts at every turn.

As always, I want to offer my loving thanks to my mother and father and to my sister, Niloo, for their sustaining presence.

Finally, I thank the people of Russia and the new republics for their openness and boldness of spirit.

—Nick Gheissari

Library of Congress Cataloging-in-Publication Data

Copyright © 1996 by Nick Gheissari

ISBN 0-9652398-0-2

Published by:
ESCOAA Images, Inc.
P.O. Box 2338
Kensington, MD 20891
USA
Phone: 1-800-840-5374 or 301-770-1971
Fax: 301-770-1988
E-mail: ESCOAA@MSN.COM
Web Address: http://www.interknowledge.com/russia/beyond

Printed by Toppan Printing Company., (Shenzhen)

Contents

Russia
—and Beyond

E VERY CREATIVE ENDEAVOR BEGINS WITH AN INSPIRATION— an epiphany—that sparks the imagination and fires a sustained passion. After the Iron Curtain rose in 1991, Nick Gheissari's photographic sojourn began with a serendipitous flight from Moscow to the city of Irkutsk in eastern Siberia. During the seven-hour flight over the wilderness, Nick met Yuri, an Irkutsk native. Clearly delighted by the young photographer's curiosity about his home province, Yuri and his wife, Lena, took Nick under their wing.

The railroad, nearly one-third of its lines powered by electricity, remains Russia's most reliable all-weather transportation system. Rail cars carry millions of passengers and thousands of tons of goods across this vast land that spans two continents, from the Bering Sea to the Baltic.

Nick went on to spend an idyllic week in and around the picturesque Irkutsk as their guest and, at their insistence, flew the 500 kilometers with them over the taiga (primeval forest) to the northernmost point of beautiful Lake Baikal. There, Nick found his passion—his "point of ecstasy." He preserved the spectacular expanse on film, and so began his quest to capture compelling images of Russia and the new republics.

Irkutsk children and their dog play on one of the boardwalks that connect the many izbas (wooden houses), where lovingly tended gardens burst forth from every patch of soft, rich earth during the brief Siberian summers. The local passion for color is then preserved—vegetables are canned; flowers are pressed—as a hopeful winter's nourishment for body and spirit.

3

Since that tumultuous summer of 1991, Nick has made nine separate trips to the countries that composed the former Soviet Union. He traveled for months at a time, seeking out the hidden places, buoyed by the kindness of newly made friends, and always, through his camera's eye, preserving the essence of these regions and the people who live within them.

At sunset, visitors stroll the great courtyard outside one of the five main State Hermitage buildings. Part of an incredible architectural heritage in the most European of Russian cities—St. Petersburg— the structures date from the late 18th- and early 19th-century reigns of Empress Elizabeth and Catherine the Great. The Winter Palace, the huge baroque centerpiece of the Hermitage and home to Russian rulers until 1917, now houses a vast and brilliant collection of Western European art.

These eloquent photographs unveil the essence of this long-shrouded land. They not only represent a thoughtful reflection of a continent's desire to experience its unfettered self but also offer a tribute to the generosity of Yuri, Lena, and all those who crossed Nick's path through *Russia and Beyond*.

Fishing trawlers from the distant shoreline town of Petropavlovsk-Kamchatsky anchor in placid Anacha Bay. This lone city center on the Far Eastern Kamchatka Peninsula—a former Soviet Pacific Fleet base—now thrives as a great fishing port, watched over in this seismic southeastern region by two active volcanoes.

*T*he looming minaret of Uleg-Beg madrasah (theological school) is one of a magnificent ensemble of three that border the ancient Registan Square (place of sand) in Samarkand, Uzbekistan. Glistening with geometric mosaics of majolica (painted tiles), the majestic madrasah was a haven for scholars seeking an enlightened curriculum during the peaceful 15th-century reign of Uleg-Beg.

Rising a monumental 100 meters to the sky, this shining titanium probe was built near the All Russia Exhibition in Moscow for the glorification of Soviet space flight achievement. Its base houses the Cosmonautics Museum, where the pioneering feats of Yuri Gagarin and Valentina Tereshkova—the first man (1961) and woman (1963) in space—are chronicled.

Atop the Kremlin's looming Saviour tower the red star glows as dusk falls on
Red Square, the center of Moscow life. To the west, against the great
Kremlin wall, rests the Lenin Mausoleum, one of the many symbols of a
rich and tumultuous past that border the square.

$\mathfrak{B}$road volcanic plateaus of the Kamchatka Crater are only accessible to wild bears and the rare human travelers who come by helicopter. The crater is part of a national park newly opened to foreigners who come to study and experience this geological hotbed of volcanoes, geysers, and steaming springs.

A retired Russian officer, living comfortably in his former far eastern duty station of Khabarovsk, dons his uniform once again—a decorated testament to his many years of service to the "supreme" Soviet. His bustling town, situated on the Amur and Ussuri rivers, now welcomes visitors and investors from a former Russian nemesis, Japan.

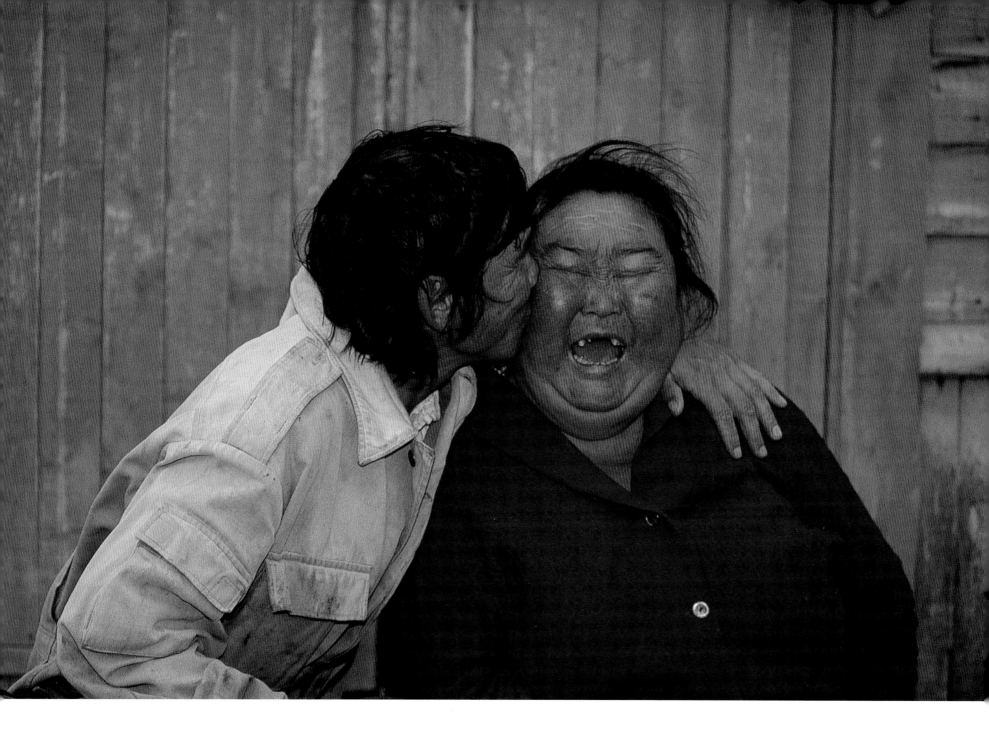

A mother is kissed by her son, and delight bursts from her face. She and her family, descendants of the Mongols, live in the Russian Amur River region near the Chinese border. Their quality of life is improving due to the establishment of the conservation-minded Amur Program, a sustainable development enterprise that receives assistance from international groups such as the Nature Conservancy and the World Wildlife Fund.

THE REGIONS—An Orientation

The former Soviet Union is a colossal landmass—an east-to-west span of two continents sprawling across eleven of the world's twenty-four time zones. By its sheer size, it seems a patient place, its glory waiting to be seen by deliberate travelers willing to take several separate journeys through four distinct regions and two mountain ranges on this double continent: Europe, Central Asia, Siberia, the Far East and Kamchatka, the Caucasus, and the Ural Mountains.

EUROPEAN REGION

This large, primarily flat and forested area includes Europe's longest river—the Volga— and comprises ten densely populated countries. The region covers a full 5.3 million square kilometers north to south, from the harsh Arctic shores to the warm waters of the Caspian Sea, and west to east from the Baltic Sea to the Ural Mountains.

European Russia—one-quarter of the Russian Federation and the largest country in Europe—forms the long north and northwestern border of the region along the Arctic Barents, Kara, and White seas. The region continues inland along boundaries with Norway, Finland, and the Baltic Sea.

The beautiful Baltic States of Estonia, Latvia, and Lithuania (and the isolated Russian Kaliningrad region) create the uneven western border with the Baltic Sea. The independent republics of Belarus, Ukraine, and Moldova share their borders west to south with Poland, the Carpathian Mountains, the Czech Republic and Slovakia, Hungary, Romania, and the subtropical waters of the Black Sea.

From south to east, the region's border is formed by the northwestern tip of the 5,000-meter-high Caucasus Mountain Range and the republics of Georgia, Armenia, and Azerbaijan, whose boundaries are shared with Turkey, Iran, and the Caspian Sea.

To the northeast, tracing the Caspian Sea, the southeastern tip of the Caucasus, and a long border with Kazakhstan, the European region completes itself with the south-to-north boundary of the low-lying (1,900 meters) Ural Mountain Range, which officially stretches more than 2,500 kilometers to reach the desolate Novaya-Zemlya islands in the Arctic seas.

THE FAR EAST AND KAMCHATKA

This region of Pacific Rim territories, stretching three million square kilometers from the Arctic Chukota to the monsoonal Primorsky Kray in the south, also includes the 1,200-kilometer-long Kamchatka Peninsula—a striking landscape containing more than 200 volcanoes and geothermic valleys.

The regional boundary encompasses big Diomede Island in the northern Chukchi Sea and wanders west and south, separating Siberia from the Far Eastern Magadan region and Khabarovsk Territory.

The border is shared with China and North Korea in the south, then heads northeast, becoming a rocky coastline along the seas of Japan and Okhotsk, finally incorporating Sakhalin Island, the formidable Kamchatka, and its Kuril Island archipelago.

SIBERIA

A gigantic, predominantly flat swath of land, fringed by mountains, Siberia covers nearly eleven million square kilometers. The region contains a staggering 1,000,000 lakes and 50,000 rivers—notably the Ob, Yenisey, and Lena—scattered throughout the four million square-kilometer taiga—the world's largest forest—and the stark tundra of the north.

From east to west, Siberia's long northern border is a complex shoreline. Its rugged peninsulas jut out into the Arctic Chukchi, East Siberian, Laptev, and Kara seas.

To the west and south, Siberia is bordered by the Ural Mountains and joins the Republic of Kazakhstan. The long southern boundary shared with Mongolia and China is punctuated by six mountain ranges, including the 4,500-meter elevations of the remote and astonishing Altay Mountains.

CENTRAL ASIA

The five republics of the Central Asian region encompass four million square kilometers of mountains, steppes, and the vast Krzyl-Kum (red sands) and Kara-Kum (black sands) deserts. From east to west, the Republic of Kazakhstan shares its long northern regional border with Russian Siberia and European Russia, whereupon, after curving south and west, it joins the Caspian Sea.

The southern border is created by the republics of Turkmenistan, Uzbekistan, Tajikistan, and Kyrgyzstan and is aided by the natural boundary of the lofty Pamir Mountain Range, which separates the region from Iran, Afghanistan, Pakistan, and China. From south to east, the Kazakh border resumes, bounded by China and the magnificent 7,000-meter Tien-Shan (mountains of heaven) range.

THE COUNTRIES
—Brief Profiles

THE RUSSIAN FEDERATION

Area: 17.1 million sq. km.
Population: 150 million
Capital: Moscow
People: 82% Russian, 4% Tatar, multiple ethnicities
Language: Russian and 100 ethnic languages
Religion: 25% Russian Orthodox, 75% Muslim, Animist, Buddhist, Jewish

[Map of the region showing countries including LITHUANIA, LATVIA, ESTONIA, BELARUS, UKRAINE, MOLDOVA, GEORGIA, ARMENIA, AZERBAIJAN, KAZAKHSTAN, TURKMENISTAN, UZBEKISTAN, KYRGYZSTAN, TAJIKISTAN, and cities including Kaliningrad, Riga, Tallinn, Murmansk, Kaunas, Vilnius, L'viv, Brest, St. Petersburg, Petrozavodsk, Minsk, Novgorod, Arkhangelsk, Chernivtsi, Kiev, Sergiev-Posad, Vologda, Chisinau, Rostov-Veliky, Yaroslavl, MOSCOW, Suzdal, Kostroma, Odessa, Vladimir, Ivanovo, Dnipropetrovsk, Kharkiv, Nizhiniy Novgorod, Kirov, Sevastopol, Simferopol, Don River, Kazan, R, Yalta, Sea of Azov, Rostov-on-Don, Volga River, Perm, Krasnodar, Volgograd, Kama River, Black Sea, Sochi, Stavropol, Yekaterinburg, Sukhumi, Tyumen, Bat'umi, Grozny, Astrakhan, Chelyabinsk, Kurgan, GEORGIA, T'bilisi, Makhachkala, Yerevan, Caspian Sea, Lake Sevan, Quba, AZERBAIJAN, Baku, Aral Sea, Khiva, Ashgabat, Lake Balkhash, Bukhara, Tashkent, Samarkand, Bishkek, Alma-Ata, Dushanbe]

ARMENIA

Area: 29,800 sq. km.
Population: 3.5 million
Capital: Yerevan
People: 90% Armenian, 10% Azeri, Russian, Kurd, Greek
Language: Armenian
Religion: Armenian Orthodox, Muslim

BELARUS

Area: 207,600 sq. km.
Population: 10.4 million
Capital: Minsk
People: 78% Belarussian, 13% Russian, 4% Polish, 3% Ukrainian
Language: Russian, Belarussian
Religion: 70% Eastern Orthodox, 20% Roman Catholic, Jewish, Protestant

GEORGIA

Area: 69,700 sq. km.
Population: 5.7 million
Capital: T'bilisi
People: 70% Georgian, 30% Armenian, Russian, Greek
Language: Russian, Georgian
Religion: Georgian Orthodox, Muslim, Russian Orthodox

AZERBAIJAN

Area: 86,600 sq. km.
Population: 7.8 million
Capital: Baku
People: 83% Azeri, 17% Tatar, Russian, Armenian, Ukrainian
Language: Azeri, Russian
Religion: Shiite Muslim, Eastern Orthodox

ESTONIA

Area: 45,000 sq. km.
Population: 1.7 million
Capital: Tallinn
People: 62% Estonian, 37% Russian, various ethnicities
Language: Estonian

KAZAKHSTAN

Area: 2.7 million sq. km.
Population: 17.4 million
Capital: Alma-Ata
People: 42% Kazakh, 37% Russian, 20% German, Ukrainian, mixed ethnicities
Language: Russian, Kazakh
Religion: Muslim, Russian Orthodox

KYRGYZSTAN

Area: 198,500 sq. km.
Population: 4.8 million
Capital: Bishkek
People: 52% Kirghiz, 48% Russian, German, Ukrainian, Tatar
Language: Kirghiz
Religion: Muslim

RUSSIA

Chukchi Sea
Wrangel Island
East Siberian Sea
Anadyr
Zemlya Frantsa-Iosifa
Severnaya Zemlya
Kara Sea
Novaya Zemlya
Laptev Sea
Novosibirskie Islands
Bering Sea
Tixi
Palana
Yarkuta
Norilsk
Shelekhov Gulf
Ob Gulf
Magadan
Lena River
Petropavlovsk-Kamchatsky
Yenisey River
Yakutsk
Sea of Okhotsk
Ob River
Angara River
Lena River
Tomsk
Novosibirsk
Kemerovo
Krasnoyarsk
Severobhikaisk
Tynda
Komsomoisk-on-Amur
Kuril Islands
Sakhalin Island
Tatar Strait
Barnaul
Yenisey River
Amur River
Amur River
Sovietskaya Gavan
Yuzhno-Sakhalinsk
Irkutsk
Lake Baikal
Chita
Argun River
Blagoveshchensk
Khabarovsk
Ulan Ude
Ussuri River
Sea of Japan
Vladivostok

TAJIKISTAN

Area: 143,100 sq. km.
Population: 6.1 million
Capital: Dushanbe
People: 65% Tajik, 35% Uzbek, Ukrainian, German, Turk, Korean
Language: Tajik
Religion: Sunni Muslim

TURKMENISTAN

Area: 448,100 sq. km.
Population: 4.3 million
Capital: Ashgabat
People: 73% Turkmen, 27% Russian, Uzbek, Kazakh, Tatar
Language: Turkmen, Russian
Religion: Muslim, Eastern Orthodox

UKRAINE

Area: 603,700 sq. km.
Population: 51.8 million
Capital: Kiev
People: 72% Ukrainian, 22% Russian, 6% Tatar, Belarussian, Moldovan, Bulgarian, Hungarian
Language: Ukrainian, Russian
Religion: Ukrainian Orthodox Church, Uniate, Roman Catholic, Eastern Orthodox, Jewish

UZBEKISTAN

Area: 447,400 sq. km.
Population: 23 million
Capital: Tashkent
People: 71% Uzbek, 29% Russian, Tajik, Kazakh, Tatar, Korean, Turk
Language: Uzbek, Russian
Religion: Sunni Muslim

LATVIA

Area: 64,600 sq. km.
Population: 2.8 million
Capital: Riga
People: 52% Latvian, 34% Russian, 14% Belarussian, various ethnicities
Language: Latvian
Religion: Lutheran, Roman Catholic, Russian Orthodox

LITHUANIA

Area: 65,200 sq. km.
Population: 3.8 million
Capital: Vilnius
People: 80% Lithuanian, 9% Russian, 8% Polish
Language: Lithuanian
Religion: Roman Catholic

MOLDOVA

Area: 33,700 sq. km.
Population: 4.5 million
Capital: Chisinau
People: 65% Moldovan/Romanian, 35% Russian, Bulgarian, Ukrainian, German
Language: Moldovan, Russian
Religion: Eastern Orthodox

UZBEKISTAN

THE ROUTES—How to Get There

RAIL

night and day train service is available from any one of nine main stations in Moscow. Rail lines extend into most of Russia and the former Soviet republics. Travelers have a choice of Elektrichky trains (suburban)— short 100- to 200-kilometer round trip—or long-distance "name trains" that journey three to four hours or more to their destinations.

The most famous of the name trains is the Trans-Siberian for Far Eastern Russia, and its segments, the Trans-Mongolian and the Trans-Manchurian for Beijing, China. The Trans-Siberian Moscow-to-Vladivostok express, the Rossia, departs from Moscow's Yaroslavl station as does the popular Moscow-to-Irkutsk line, the Baikal Express.

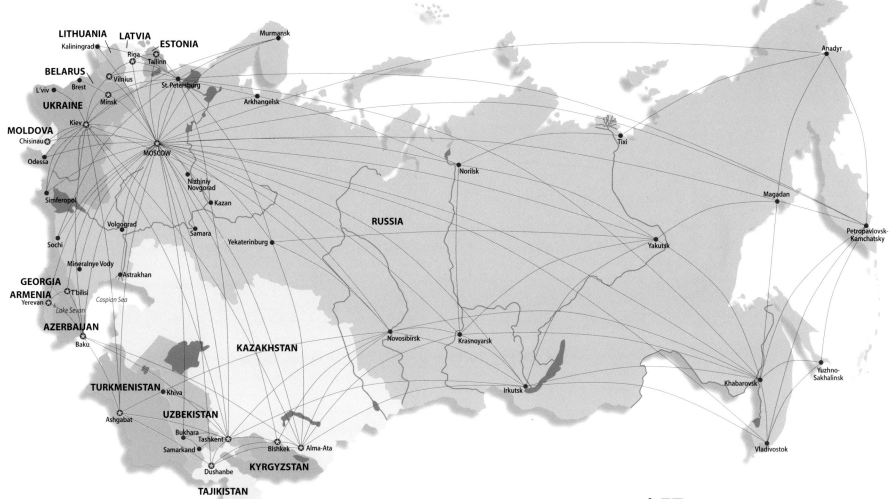

LITHUANIA
LATVIA
ESTONIA
BELARUS
UKRAINE
MOLDOVA
GEORGIA
ARMENIA
AZERBAIJAN
TURKMENISTAN
UZBEKISTAN
KYRGYZSTAN
TAJIKISTAN
KAZAKHSTAN
RUSSIA

Kaliningrad
Riga
Tallinn
Vilnius
L'viv
Brest
Minsk
Kiev
Chisinau
Odessa
Simferopol
Sochi
Mineralnye Vody
T'bilisi
Yerevan
Lake Sevan
Caspian Sea
Baku
Khiva
Ashgabat
Bukhara
Tashkent
Samarkand
Dushanbe
Bishkek
Alma-Ata
Murmansk
St. Petersburg
Arkhangelsk
MOSCOW
Nizhiniy Novgorad
Kazan
Volgograd
Samara
Astrakhan
Yekaterinburg
Novosibirsk
Krasnoyarsk
Irkutsk
Norilsk
Tixi
Anadyr
Magadan
Yakutsk
Petropavlovsk-Kamchatsky
Khabarovsk
Yuzhno-Sakhalinsk
Vladivostok

AIR

Various European, Asian, and North American airlines serve destinations in the Russian Federation and the fourteen autonomous republics. In addition, round-trip flights to, and connections out of, Russia and the new republics originate from each of Moscow's four airports. Distances within the Central Asian region, especially, are best traveled by air.

TIME ZONES

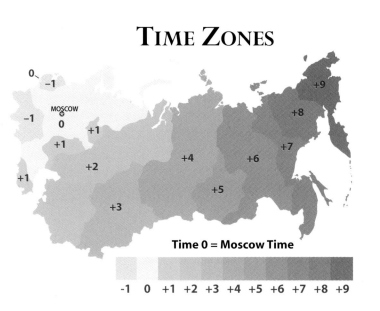

0
−1
MOSCOW
0
−1
+1
−1
+1
+2
+1
+3
+4
+5
+6
+7
+8
+9

Time 0 = Moscow Time

−1 0 +1 +2 +3 +4 +5 +6 +7 +8 +9

RECREATION

Opportunities for year-round outdoor recreation are becoming more abundant among the countries of the former Soviet Union. In European Russia, hiking, rock climbing, whitewater rafting, and downhill and cross-country skiing are available in the Middle Urals and at the mountaintop resorts of Dombay and the superb Pri-Elbrus in the Caucasus.

The Baltic States offer acres of virgin forests designated for hunting, and networks of rivers and lakes for yachting, fishing, and canoeing. From Estonia to Lithuania, lovely beaches grace the coastlines of Riga Bay and the Baltic Sea.

The Black Sea resorts of Ukraine, Russia, and Georgia boast some of the finest swimming beaches in the world.

In Far Eastern Russia, the volcanic Kamchatka Peninsula is a paradise for hikers, climbers, and anglers. Planning ahead is necessary—helicopters must be chartered for trips to the interior.

WATERWAYS

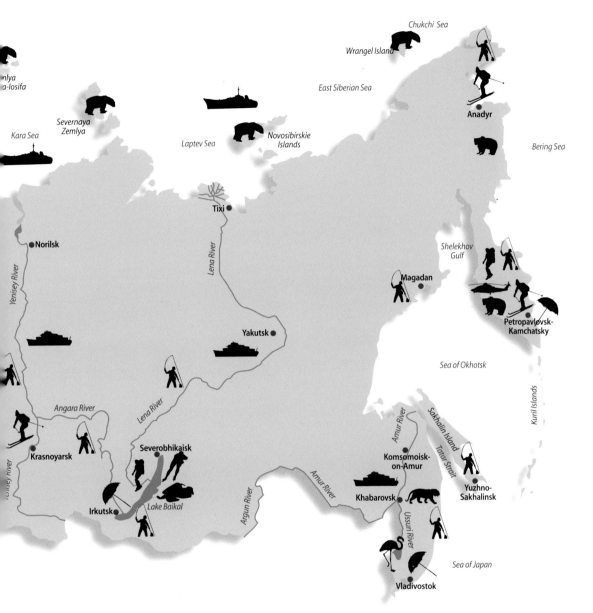

A gentler reflection on the regions can be had by cruising from city to city on the myriad of canals, rivers, and lakes. Summer boats from Moscow to St. Petersburg follow the Moscow Canal to the Volga River, passing several Golden Ring towns along the way, and then proceed north through lakes and reservoirs to the tsarist capital.

The leisurely fourteen-day Volga River cruise—from Moscow to Astrakhan, passing through the Volga Delta to the Caspian Sea—docks at nine cities en route.

In Siberia, Lena River cruises from the city of Yakutsk to the Arctic Laptev Sea offer a priceless vantage point. Ten-day summer excursions on the Far Eastern Amur River sail along the Chinese border and stop at the bustling Russian city of Khabarovsk before reaching the Pacific Ocean.

LAKE BAIKAL

To hike the pristine wilderness around the 636-kilometer-long Lake Baikal is a wonderful adventure—80 percent of the more than 2,000 known plant and animal species are exclusive to the region. On an island in the northern end of the 2,500-year-old lake live the nerpa—the only freshwater seals in the world. Fishing is incomparable in these crystal-clear waters, where more than fifty species flourish, including sturgeon and a popular local delicacy, the omul.

19

European Region

The most familiar of the regions, this huge area—European Russia, Estonia, Latvia, Lithuania, Belarus, Ukraine, Moldova, Georgia, Armenia, and Azerbaijan—offers an extravagance of history and culture.

Moscow, the northern European seat of political and spiritual power for all Russians, was preceded in its greatness by the 9th-century settlement of Novgorod (new town) and the fabled Golden Ring—a circle of charming old Kremlin towns, including Suzdal, Rostov, and Kostroma. On the Gulf of Finland further north, the glorious tsarist city of St. Petersburg was created by and for Russia's royal families.

Heroic and brilliantly gilded statues adorn a fountain along the expansive mall—2 kilometers long—of the All Russia Exhibition Center. Formerly the USSR Economic Achievement Exhibition, its architecture and promenades were designed exclusively to celebrate all things Soviet. Today, it is a retail enterprise featuring merchandise from all over the world.

Through lacy winter branches near
the banks of the Moscow River rises
the imposing five-domed Smolensk
Cathedral, stationed on the grounds of
Novodevichy (new maidens) Convent
and Cemetery. At one time the
convent, a cloistered prison for ladies
of noble birth, became a convenient
place of banishment for the difficult
half-sister of Peter the Great. Today,
winter revelers sled the hillside
outside the convent walls, oblivious to
its complex history and the famous
Russian citizens entombed there.

Further west, the captivating medieval Baltic capitals of Tallinn, Riga, and Vilnius reflect many centuries of multiple occupations by the Swedes, Poles, Germans, and Russians.

To the south lie the re-emerging Belarussian capital of Minsk, the beautiful 9th-century tree-filled Ukrainian capital of Kiev—the Mother City of Eastern Slavs—and, beyond the Carpathian Mountains amidst the age-old vineyards of Turk-influenced Moldova (springs of water), the capital city of Chisinau.

Further south and east, the city-resorts of the Black Sea—Odessa, Yalta, Dagomys, and Sochi, are still havens for politicos and poets. Eastward, the perennial beauty of the Don and Volga River regions belies a history of invasions by the infamous Tatar "Golden Horde" from across the Caucasus Mountains.

Below the steep slopes of the Southern Caucasus, the Georgian "Riviera" town of Sukhumi earned its health spa reputation during the Roman conquests. Landlocked Armenia and its neighbor, Azerbaijan, on the western shores of the Caspian Sea, were at one time part of the Turkish and Persian empires.

Further north and east, the Ural Mountains—once crossed by merchants, Russian armies, tsarist emissaries, and gulag prisoners—now simply serve as a traveler's gateway to the interminable Siberia and the Far East.

23

oscow's 150-station underground Metro system (and World War II bomb shelter) is the world's largest, with nine million passengers daily. The Metro doubles as a lavish showcase for public art: gilded friezes, massive statuary, stained glass, chandeliers, and mosaics of Russian and Ukrainian history grace the cavernous vaults of the central city stations.

The spirits of Pavlova, Nijinsky, Nureyev, and Chaliapin dwell within the beloved Bolshoi (large) Theater. A stunning venue for both the renowned Bolshoi Ballet company and the Moscow Opera, its rich legacy is reflected in the opulent six-tiered hall of crimson and gold. Looking to the future under new direction, the Bolshoi promises to introduce a more eclectic and original collection of dance and opera performances to its devoted audiences.

S t. Basil's Cathedral, with its distinctive Russian design of riotously colored onion domes and gables, beckons like a holy dream on the southern edge of Red Square. The structure was officially named Pokrovsky (intercession) Cathedral to commemorate the 16th-century conquest of Kazan by the reviled Tsar Ivan the Terrible. Its unofficial name was lovingly bestowed to honor the canonized Vasily (Basil) the Blessed, a clairvoyant who "saw" Ivan's demise. Nearby, a Russian folk ensemble, as colorfully attired as the cathedral, sings the tale of Vasily—the holy fool—for the many visitors who cross the square.

Enthusiastic free enterprise thrives on the city streets and in Moscow's Izmaylovsky Park, as vendors sell everything from exquisite hand-made Bukhara rugs to "tea-cozy" dolls dressed in cheerful folk costumes. An open-air market informality prevails, and prices are what the buyer and seller agree between them.

Art students in the Golden Ring town of Kostroma, northeast of Moscow, enjoy an outdoor museum of unique 16th-century wooden structures, including this elongated church on stilts. In the distance, the great golden domes of the monastery of St. Ipaty rise above the trees. Built by the Godunov dynasty, it boasts a splendid interior filled with 17th-century frescoes created by a noted group of Kostroma painters who traveled the Golden Ring plying their trade.

Beautiful little Suzdal, the former center of culture and trade for the medieval Golden Ring towns, lies peaceful and protected in all its 12th-century rural glory by Russian Federation mandate and by the pure snows that accent its exceptional Russian architecture. A senior resident, who has seen his share of history, walks past one of the more than thirty churches built by wealthy merchants who prospered here during the 17th and 18th centuries.

Colorfully faceted domes crown the Church of the Resurrection of Christ, which elegantly presides over the spectacular city of St. Petersburg. Inspired by St. Basil's cathedral in Moscow, the church was built on the very spot where, in 1881, terrorists assassinated the reform-minded Tsar Alexander II. Today, the site is also known as the Church of the Saviour on the Spilled Blood.

The Anichkov Palace, bordering the Fontanka River Canal and Nevsky Prospekt in St. Petersburg, served as one of the many guest houses of Catherine the Great, who extended her long-term hospitality to favored friends as well as her lover and champion, Grigory Potemkin. Visitors approach the palace on the Anichkov Bridge, its four corners decorated with the famous landmark statues of horse tamers.

St. Petersburg, the former capital of Russia, is often called the Venice of the North. Founded on the swampy shores of the Gulf of Finland and the River Neva, the city features a network of bridges, canals, and beautifully carved stone embankments. During the summer, visitors are treated to "City on the Neva" cruises embarking from the Hermitage, short canal excursions, and hydrofoil sailings to Petrodvorets, Tsar Peter's "Russian Versailles."

Along Freedom Street, the red-roofed houses and guildhalls of old-town Riga, Latvia, reflect the city's prosperous past and German, Dutch, and Swedish influences. Cars are banned from the city center, where visitors can explore such exquisite structures as the Blackhead Brotherhood—a 13th-century meeting hall that catered to bachelor merchants of the time and was named for one of its three patron saints, Mauritius, who was black.

On a winter's eve, the lights of Riga are reflected in the River Daugava on which vessels regularly cruise the five miles to Riga Bay and the Baltic Sea. According to town lore, the unusual suspension bridge is unofficially named "Voss's Guitar" after a pre-1991 communist politico who had the span constructed to expedite his trips to a vacation home.

ozy fairy lights, a popular home ornament, brighten the spirits during the long dark Baltic winters. This Russian family in Riga formally poses before receiving old friends into their tiny apartment, where they will share the requisite vodka, meat pastries, and music as they welcome the New Year. Preparation for the party required a full day of shopping in the five 1930s-vintage Zeppelin hangars— one for each food group—of the sprawling Riga Market, Europe's largest.

A couple walks the grounds of Castle Hill, a 14th-century fortress settlement overlooking the Neris River and the winterscape of Vilnius, Lithuania. The oldest settlement in the city, its ruins became a symbol of the Lithuanian independence movement of the late 1980s when the traditional tricolor was at last raised on its parapets. Just south of Castle Hill, a young woman pauses beneath a statue in the facade of the beautiful Vilnius Cathedral.

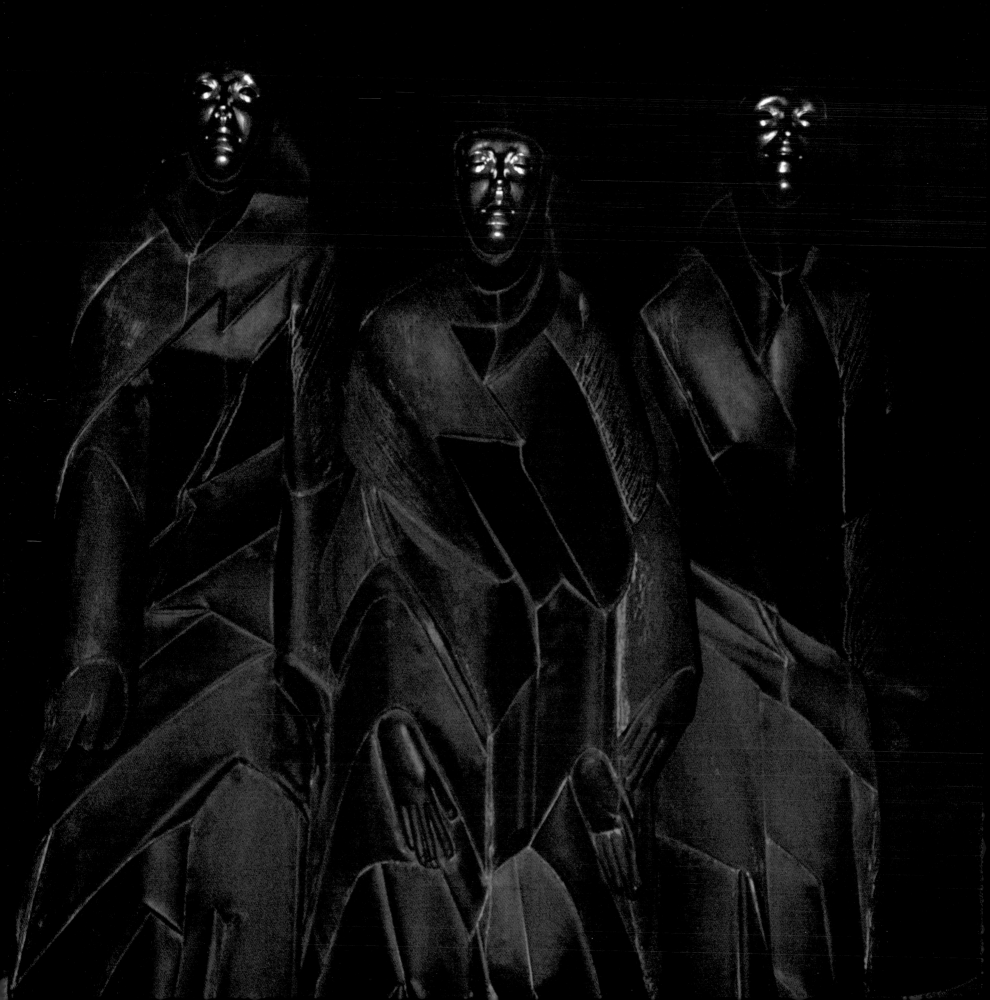

In Vilnius, a statue of the 19th-century Polish-Lithuanian writer Adam Mickiewicz graces the grounds of the Gothic 15th-century Monastery of the Bernardines—a Polish order—and the lovely red-brick St. Anne's church, which cast its spell even on Napoleon. In the center of the city, the three burnished gold faces of Tragedy, Comedy, and Drama emerge from a black alcove above the entrance to the City Theater—one of Vilnius's many live performance venues.

T he huge glass and concrete Republican Exhibition Center is a landmark
for newly cosmopolitan Minsk, Belarus, which lies on the Strislach River.
Formerly the Byelorussian Exhibition of Economic Achievements, the
center now features regular international trade fairs as testament to the city's
phoenix-like ability to transcend its horrific World War II history and dreary Soviet
industrial reputation. The pride of the new Minsk shows on the face of a war
veteran, who survived the extermination of more than half the city's population.

47

The Baroque 18th-century Mariyinsky Palace in Ukraine's capital city of Kiev was built in 1742 for Empress Elizabeth, daughter of Peter the Great. Destroyed during World War II, the palace was restored in 1950 to its former glory. Today, the turquoise, blue, and yellow structure sits in a beautiful area known as Lipke (linden trees), and serves as a perfect setting for presidential receptions. In the center of Kiev, a statue honoring the city's legendary Scandinavian founders casts a bold silhouette against the evening sky.

The Swallow's Nest, a tiny castle built by a German oil magnate in 1912, and, nearby, a beautifully preserved 19th-century cathedral, are but two of hundreds of architectural gems that perch on the rugged cliffs above the famous Black Sea beaches. Today, the Swallow's Nest is a restaurant, catering to visitors who enjoy the posh mineral spring resorts in the area and swim in the warm summer waters within sight of the snow-covered Caucasus Mountain Range. Vacationers enjoy the fruits of the region—figuratively and literally. The foothills are thick with vineyards and lemon, tangerine, pomegranate, and persimmon orchards.

Sochi, a favorite Black Sea resort established in the 1930s, features an extensive array of large hotels and health spas. Its subtropical climate, lovely parks, and avenues of cypress, palm, and magnolia soothe the weariest of travelers. Farther north on the Crimean beaches of Yalta, crowds of sun worshipers absorb some of the advertised 2,200 hours of sun per year at this "Russian Riviera." The benevolent Yalta climate has also drawn its share of prominent figures, including the peace-talking world leaders of the 1945 Yalta Summit and tubercular playwright and physician Anton Chekov, who lived out his last years in the Crimean vineyards.

The Caucasus

Horses descended from the great herds of the Cossacks graze the Kuban Steppe, just north of the Caucasus Mountain Range. These plains served as a staging area for the Russian army and the native Kuban Cossacks (freemen or horsemen) during the 18th-century routs of the Caucasus tribes—some of whom sought refuge in the daunting 3,000- to 5,000-meter elevations of their ruggedly beautiful home.

The tiny 1,500-meter-high Dombay resort area, in the Teberdinsky Nature Reserve, nestles below the spectacular central Caucasus range and offers year-round outdoor recreation. Summer hiking, rock climbing, whitewater rafting, and December-to-June skiing are exhilarating pursuits in these striking altitudes. Helicopters ferry the more adventurous to the higher ski slopes or to nearby glaciers—several of the more than 2,000 ice floes in the Caucasus.

Two descendants of the Caucasus tribes—an elder from the northwest Kabarda peoples and a woman from the northeast mountain kingdom of Dagestan— radiate the vibrance of a life in the mountains. Their hardy constitutions are testimonials to the benefits of the mineral water springs that percolate throughout the region.

Quaint houses, protected by meticulously decorated courtyard gates, brighten the winter streets of this Caucasus village. Outside one of the gates, a resident waits for a ride to the train station. There she will embark on a rejuvenating trip to the town of Mineralnye Vody (mineral water) where the myriad of spas and sanatoria serve up the highly touted and healthful waters of the Caucasus Mountains.

A wooden house, painted the traditional Russian blue and accented by weatherbeaten white shutters, sits peacefully in the Volga River Delta region near the city of Astrakhan, 100 kilometers from the Caspian Sea. The region, where the Volga branches into 800 tributaries, is known as the Astrakhan State Biosphere Reserve—a botanical, marine, and zoological paradise.

 father's Tatar and Mongol ancestry, as well as his livelihood, is passed on to his son—
he fishes the rich waters of the Volga-Astrakhan region and offers boat taxi service to
visitors traveling to village destinations on the hundreds of delta waterways.

On the shores of the Caspian Sea, a pleased fisherman rests after casting his nets from sunrise until noon. Nearby, an Azerbaijani woman harvests the precious roe from his daily catch of sturgeon. Her livelihood, once assured by the local and global demand for the coveted black beluga or rare golden sterlet caviars, may now be threatened by the chronic poaching that has occurred since the breakup of the Soviet Union—though steps are being taken to prevent these excesses.

wo young boys maneuver their small craft through the complex network of tributaries in the Volga Delta. On shore, an amused resident pauses in front of her house.

Ural Mountains

A cloud hovers above a rocky clearing in the Ural Mountains, the traditional boundary between European Russia and Siberia. White moss, wild blueberries, and mushrooms proliferate in these relatively low altitudes of blunt, mineral-rich rock formations. In the middle Ural foothills, life moves slowly in a peaceful settlement where home fires burn and woodpiles are well stocked in preparation for the long, hard winters.

A family group in the Ural town of Yekaterinburg (named for Catherine the Great), proudly poses at the bottom of a little hill near the indigenous log house they've occupied for many happy years. Another family, the Romanovs, was exiled to Yekaterinburg during the Russian Revolution, and all—Tsar Nicholas, Tsarina Alexandra, and their five children—were eventually executed in 1918 by their Bolshevik guards.

1n Krasnaturinsk, a man ends a day's work in his large dacha (summer house) garden and looks
forward to the luxury of spending several hours at the public banya (bath). Across town, a
young girl strikes a puckish pose in the courtyard of her apartment building.

Domes

"...Suddenly in the silence fell
Once more the distant tolling bell
And all was lucid in no time..."

—Mikhail Lermontov

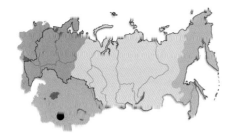

Central Asia

In centuries past, the primarily Muslim republics of Central Asia— Kazakhstan, Turkmenistan, Uzbekistan, Tajikistan, and Kyrgyzstan—thrived on the wealth of goods brought by camel caravans crossing to and from China on the plains and deserts of the Great Silk Route. The expansive steppes in the north—also traversed by Kazakh horsemen and their antecedents, the Mongol hordes—later served as an embarkation point for another journey: the first manned space flight of Yuri Gagarin.

Mythic Samarkand, Uzbekistan—the "Eden of the East"—has maintained its magnificent beauty despite 2,500 years of plunder and revolution.

Marco Polo once traveled the region surrounding the lovely 19th-century Kazakh capital of Alma-Ata—an area sheltered by the tremendous Tien-Shan Mountain Range, which extends into, and covers most of, neighboring Kyrgyzstan. Here, in the higher elevations, snow leopards, bears, and small goat-like antelope—or chamois—thrive.

In southernmost Turkmenistan, 80 percent of the country is blanketed by the Kara-Kum Desert. Early Turkmen nomads traveled this barren stretch of land to transport their newly woven, rich, red carpets to the Bukhara Bazaar in Uzbekistan. Today, sought-after Bukhara carpets (Turkmenian carpets to the weavers) are renowned worldwide.

Just east, in heavily populated Uzbekistan, the romantic cities of Tashkent,

Bukhara, and Samarkand are a visual feast—ancient mosques and madrasahs, from the legendary reign of Tamerlane, still stand amidst modern, more utilitarian architecture.

All but 10 percent of tiny Tajikistan is covered by the great 7,400-meter Pamir (roof of the world) Mountains—part of a series of ranges that include the Himalayas and that, long ago, gave inspiration to native poet Omar Khayyám.

Vendors offer the fruits of their labors at the Trade Cupolas in the modern, verdant city of Tashkent, Uzbekistan. Growers from all over the countryside gather to sell produce and material made from their most important crop, cotton. Uzbeki cotton exports are the world's largest, and, in the center of Tashkent's Teatralnaya (theater) Square, a large, bronze cotton-ball fountain celebrates this symbol of Uzbeki prosperity.

This old man's peculiar combination of native garb and modern dress does not diminish his ancient Tatar countenance. Walking through the equally ancient city of Bukhara, he proudly wears a relic from the more recent past, a medal from the Soviet government. Nearby, a young mother and her daughters pose in their khalats (silk dresses and pantaloons) and sweaters, warmed by the sun against the autumn chill of the desert air.

1n Bukhara,
Uzbekistan, the
clear gaze of a
Muslim elder holds all
the mysteries of Holy
Islam. He takes tea at the
chaikhane (tea house)
near the Liabi-Khauz
Mosque and Madrasahs,
one of the few remaining
ensembles from the over
100 madrasahs and 300
mosques of this once

holiest of cities. A sublime oasis on the edge of the Krzyl-Kum Desert, Bukhara has also seen its share of horror. Its ancient rulers delighted in flinging prisoners into a hole of rats, snakes, and scorpions or off the 47-meter-tall Kalyan minaret. Today, the "Bug Pit" and "Tower of Death" are tourist attractions.

A cable car rises slowly above the gorgeous capital city of Alma-Ata (father of apples), Kazakhstan. The young city is surrounded by terraced apple orchards in the foothills of the Tien-Shan Mountain Range—with peaks taller than both the European Alps and North American ranges. Alma-Atans take great pleasure in the beautiful sights of their city. Two Russian soldiers and a young Kazakh peer tour one of the many graceful, tree-lined boulevards.

Faces

"*I am thrown into life,*
which carries the streams
Of the race down the
stream of decades..."
— Boris Pasternak

89

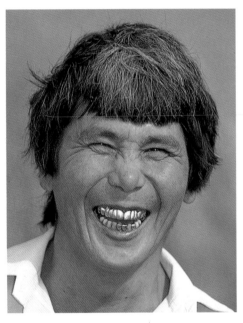

Siberia

Siberia, the great Siber (sleeping land) Plain, is today split into two huge sub-regions— from the Ural Mountains east to the western borders of the Pacific territories with the winding south-to-north Yenisey River as the dividing line. Its name connotes cold desolation, lifelong banishment, and the gulags. However, despite its dubious past, the region offers a breathtaking beauty.

In the 16th century, Siberia was first given over—under duress—to Tsar Ivan the Terrible by the Tatars, who occupied the region. Later, pioneer merchants and their Cossack protectors, sanctioned

Dazzling Lake Baikal, the sacred Blue Eye of eastern Siberia, revered for its mile-deep mysteries, extraordinary species, and crystalline waters, is the oldest freshwater lake on the planet.

by the Tsar, moved into the flat lowlands of the west and established trading posts extending from the tundra to the taiga. Throughout the 16th and 17th centuries, the great push east continued—indigenous tribal resistance and errant Tatar uprisings were quashed to protect the highly profitable fur trade—and Siberia became fully Russian.

Today, most of the population has settled into the southern cities along the west-to-east Trans-Siberian Railroad. The astounding Moscow-to-Vladivostok line was painstakingly constructed from 1891 to 1917, using the hard labor of Chinese, convicts, and exiles. Several of the rail towns, originally founded as trading

A wizened babushka in the Siberian city of Irkutsk passes through the gate of her gaily adorned wooden house. Behind the blue fence, her garden grows as it has for the past sixty summers of her eighty years. Further east, in the city of Krasnoyarsk, a daughter shares an affectionate moment with her father as her family prepares for Sunday supper in the dining room of their dacha.

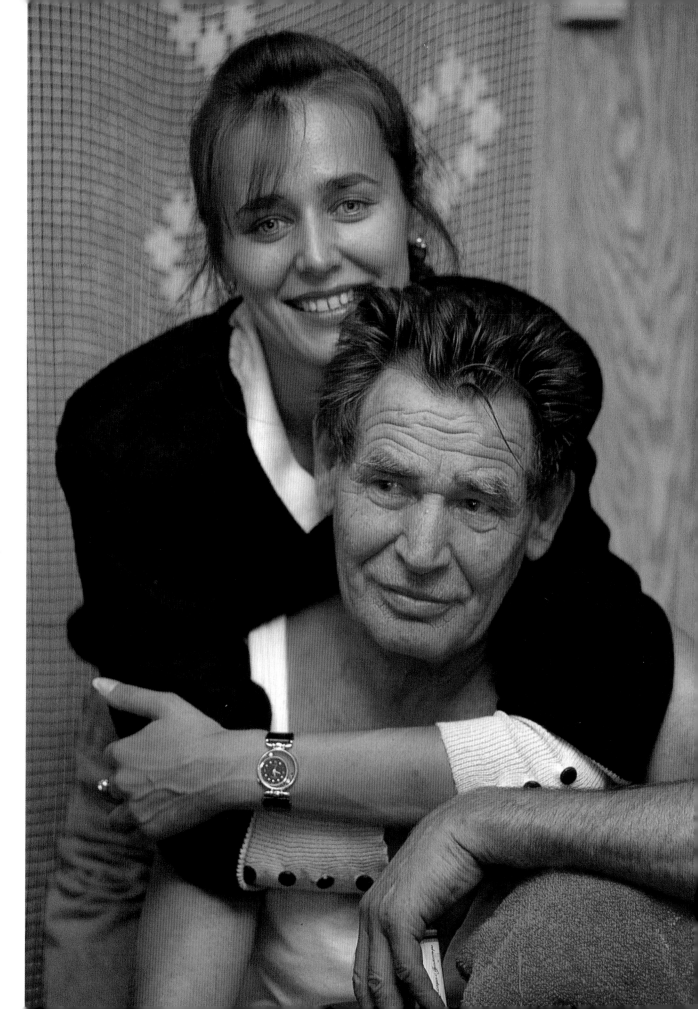

posts or Cossack garrisons, are preservers of the history in this remote region.

Irkutsk, the 19th-century Paris of Siberia situated near mountains, the taiga, and marvelous Lake Baikal, is undoubtedly the most fascinating city on the Trans-Siberian line. The town traces its culture back to an exiled aristocracy who maintained a highly educated society and, for a time, resisted the Red Tide of the Russian Revolution.

The Lena River, which originates near the northwestern tip of Lake Baikal, flows north through the tundra of the Sakha Territory. There the indigenous Evenk and Chukchi peoples still hunt, as they have for centuries, during the summer White Nights near the Arctic Laptev Sea.

To reach Moscow, this young Krasnoyarsk family will spend many days traveling two-thirds of the 9,000 kilometers on the "Great Siberian"—the Trans-Siberian Railway. The line, indisputably the longest operational track on the globe, originates on the Pacific Coast at the End of the World Station in Vladivostok. Also in Krasnoyarsk, these youngsters play in a small tar-paper shanty that huddles in the play yard of their Soviet-style apartment building. The girls pretend the hut is their own dacha in the southern Siberian countryside.

A young woman gazes over the graceful hills and striking rock formations of Stolby (pillars) Nature Reserve near the city of Krasnoyarsk on the Yenisey River. Further east, on the road from Irkutsk that extends to the southern tip of Lake Baikal, stands the pristine reconstruction of 15th- to-19th-century Siberian izbas (wooden houses) and churches known as the Museum of Wooden Architecture.

utside the city of Krasnoyarsk, a delightful cluster of Siberian dachas clings to a hillside covered with May gardens. A local resident, elegantly clad in parka and fedora, passes by the trademark houses on his way to work.

Windows

"Our modest country house,
Those places where I used to see…
…Happiness was so close then,
So simple…"

—Alexander Pushkin

The Far East and Kamchatka

The territories of the Pacific Rim and the Kamchatka Peninsula provide some of the most spectacular topography in Russia, as well as several of its most unusual cities.

In the southernmost territory of Primorsky Kray the city of Vladivostok—"The Lord of the East"— sits on the hilly vistas overlooking Golden Horn Bay. Home to the Russian Pacific Fleet since 1860, the city seeks to transform itself into a cosmopolitan Asian capital to rival Hong Kong.

Five young fishermen troll a small tributary that feeds the powerful Amur River, the longest waterway in Far Eastern Russia. Once possessed by the Cossacks, the Amur forms part of the turbulent Russian-Chinese border.

In the north, above the confluence of the Ussuri and Amur rivers, the lively city of Khabarovsk has jettisoned its image as a strategic military base guarding the Chinese border. The city now prefers to welcome trade and tourism from both China and Japan.

Much further north, past rugged, oil-rich Sakhalin Island, sits Magadan, the infamous acquisition port for the 1930s Stalinist slave force—five million of whom died working the Kolyma gold mines.

Across the Sea of Okhotsk, the imposing Kamchatka Peninsula looms, a breathtaking landscape of constant volcanic and geothermic activity. Discovered in the 17th century by a Cossack explorer, Kamchatka metamorphosed into a missile testing range—off limits until 1990. Today, the 1,000-kilometer-long peninsula is open to travelers who wish to explore its boiling Valley of Geysers and more than 200 volcanoes, and also its forests and fertile grassy plains that sustain thousands of brown bears and sable.

Accompanied by balalaikas and accordions, a brightly costumed dance troupe performs on the aft deck of an Amur River cruise ship. Also on the cruise, a young girl dons her jeweled hat and joins in the spirit of the moment while watching a second dance performance at sunset.

An ambitious young Amur River fisherman displays his morning catch. Upriver, the popular Tower Kafe and Casino sit high above the beach at the edge of the City Park in Khabarovsk. Silhouetted against the evening sky, the statue of the 19th-century founder of Khabarovsk, Count Muravev-Amursky, presides over its watery namesake.

A young Nanai tribeswoman, whose people have inhabited the Amur River region for centuries, pauses in her finery before performing her tribal stories through dance and song. In Khabarovsk, veterans of long-ago World War II campaigns exchange their stories over cigarettes and vodka, following a commemorative luncheon. Each man proudly wears layers of medals given by the centralized government that lasted almost three-quarters of a century.

One of the many awe-inspiring sopky (volcanoes) protruding from the landscape of the Kamchatka Peninsula lies dormant—for now. Capped by a barren deposit of silt inside its crater, the sleeping giant waits for a cue sent by the shifting plates of the Pacific Rim.

115

Houses pepper the lush hillsides of Petropavlovsk-Kamchatsky where the fertile volcanic soils consistently produce outsized vegetables, including the giant green cabbages common to the area. Close to town, bathers gather around the plentiful thermal pools to absorb health-giving minerals.

116

In this daunting wilderness, the seldom-seen Kamchatkan brown bears, the largest of their species, are nourished by the huge salmon spawned in heated rivers, and by the ruby-red berries that proliferate in the region.

Standing upright,
slightly askance from human view,
soul upon soul creates its own meaning,
speaks out loud on the mystery of life.

—Richard Swoboda